The First Pentecostal Anglican

Anglican

The Life and Legacy of Alexander Boddy

Gavin Wakefield

Director of Mission and Pastoral Studies, Cranmer Hall, Durham

GROVE BOOKS LIMITED
RIDLEY HALL RD CAMBRIDGE CB3 9HU

Contents

Acknowledgements

I would like to thank Mark Cartledge for his encouragement to learn about Alexander Boddy, and Desmond Cartwright and William Kay for reading a draft and providing helpful comments. Thanks also to Fran for tolerating another enthusiasm.

The Cover Illustration is by Peter Ashton

First Impression October 2001
ISSN 1470-8531
ISBN 1 85174 480 0

1
Preparation for Pentecost[1]

Many Pentecostals take pride in knowing their history and so have been more likely than Anglicans to know about the Vicar of Monkwearmouth, Sunderland of a century ago. Alexander Alfred Boddy is regarded by Pentecostal historians as the father of British Pentecostalism, and he was a key player in the European Pentecostal Movement prior to the First World War. Many dramatic and powerful events, prefiguring charismatic renewal, healing services, large scale teaching conventions and Toronto Blessing phenomena, took place in his own church hall.

Boddy was no one-dimensional character, but a seasoned traveller and writer, a committed Anglican who had a big ecumenical heart, concerned to do something about the harsh conditions of the workers in his parish, and a man of prayer who was passionate about helping Christians to live holy lives in the power of God's Spirit.

His Early Life

Alexander Boddy was born on 15th November 1854, the third son of Rev'd James Boddy, a Rector in Cheetham, Manchester. His mother was Jane Vazeille Stocks, a descendant of Mary Vazeille whose second husband had been John Wesley. The family link was clearly valued for the second son was named Herbert Anthony Vazeille, and later Alexander was to give the Vazeille name to his daughters. According to Boddy's own account he was a poorly baby and expected to die: 'But the Lord raised me up again when death seemed certain.'[2] One suspects he might have seen this as divine providence, saving him for a significant purpose, perhaps similar to John Wesley's experience of being saved as a young boy from a burning house.

He was educated at Manchester Grammar School and then articled to solicitors in Manchester at the age of 17 in 1871. He appreciated this time: 'My seven years in the law brought me face to face with the seamy side of life and made me perhaps most sympathetic with the tempted.'[3] However, he went through a spiritual crisis which altered his career. The testimony of his daughter Jane would suggest that this crisis occurred through a visit to the Keswick Holiness Convention.[4] As a result he decided to follow his father James and his brother Herbert by seeking ordination in the Church of England.

1   See Martin Robinson *The Charismatic Anglican—Historical and Contemporary. A Comparison of Alexander Boddy and Michael C Harper* M. Litt. Thesis University of Birmingham 1976, chapter 2.
2   'Some Sacred Memories' *Confidence* 7.2, 1914, p 23. Note the format for numbering *Confidence* varies over the years.
3   'From Sunderland to Pittington' *Confidence* 132, 1923, p 66.
4   See her memoir at the Donald Gee Centre for Pentecostal and Charismatic Research.

Ordained Ministry

After studying at the University of Durham, in 1880 he was ordained deacon by Bishop J B Lightfoot of Durham and first went to be Curate to his sick father. His father died early in 1881. He was then moved to be Curate at St Helen's, Low Fell, Gateshead. He stayed there for three years and was briefly Curate at St Helen's, Bishop Auckland in 1884.[5]

Moving to Auckland brought him into closer contact with the Bishop who took a personal interest in the development of his curates—often called 'Lightfoot's Lambs.' Boddy was selected by the Bishop for the parish of All Saints, Monkwearmouth, where he was to spend most of his life. It had been in a bad way almost since its formation in 1844, with its Vicar turned to drink, repeated lawsuits against him, and a tiny congregation.[6] The Vicar refused to resign, so Boddy was appointed initially as Curate, becoming Vicar two years later on the death of the incumbent.

His early ministry was based round prayer, individual and corporate, pastoral care of all in need, evangelistic campaigns, and a steady pattern of Prayer Book services. As the work and the population grew, another church, St Aidan's, was built at Roker, and a parish hall on Fulwell Road. This hall later became the venue of the Sunderland Whitsuntide Conventions.

His pastoral concern is well illustrated by his action in 1892 during a prolonged miners' strike. Within his parish many hundreds of ironworkers were laid off because of the strike. Boddy raised £500 for the workers and their families. This was much appreciated and after the strike he was presented with a silver communion set and urn which he continued to treasure many years later.[7] The YMCA published a glowing account of the man. His passion for unity was noted, for he had a 'catholicity of Spirit and a deep spirituality of mind.' He was seen as combining the best of several traditions, for he 'seeks to combine church order with evangelistic zeal.' He was said to hold three prayer meetings each week, to support Church Army work in his parish and to be a devoted Bible teacher.[8]

The Character of the Man

Boddy seems to have had a restless and curious streak from an early age: he began foreign travel as a young clerk, saving half his lunch money each day until he had sufficient funds to visit Paris![9] Over the next 20 years his travels took him further afield, touring western Europe in 1876. He later went to Sweden, Russia, North Africa, Canada and the USA, and on two visits to the Middle East and the Holy Land. He wrote five travel books and a devo-

---

5 His entry in successive Crockford's does not mention the Bishop Auckland post, but it can be found in *The Clergy List* of the time.
6 All Saints, Sunderland, *Centenary Magazine* 1944, p 17.
7 'From Sunderland to Pittington' *Confidence*132, 1923, p 66.
8 'Rev Alex A Boddy FRGS' *YMCA Flashes*, Vol 11, No 8, 1895, p 86.
9 Jane Boddy, *Letter*, p 1.

tional book on the Holy Land, gaining a number of honours for his travel writing. These books provide glimpses of the character of the man and hints about his theological understanding.

First of all, his adventurous spirit stands out. He did not always follow the well trodden paths, preferring to make his own way, often without interpreters and with only rudimentary knowledge of the local language.[10] He was very conscious of following in the steps of the earlier explorers.[11]

Secondly, he was at ease with people from a wide spectrum of social backgrounds, equally at home gaining assistance from the Russian Governor Prince Golitsin and in learning 'Russian country expressions' from peasant women in the third class accommodation on a river steamer. He astonished the first class passengers by helping those in third class in loading logs for the fuel, their means of paying their way on the trip.[12] He tried to visit those in prison and once spent a few minutes alone, locked up in one of the worst cells.[13]

Thirdly, his travels brought him into contact with Christians of many traditions. At home he was open to Christians of non-conformist denominations, especially Methodists. On his foreign journeys he met amongst others Copts, Presbyterians, Roman Catholics and the Orthodox. He showed them great respect, but believed the purpose of co-operation with other Christians was to advance missionary work.[14] Whilst abroad he regularly visited Church Missionary Society (CMS) missionaries, and shared his faith whenever he could.

His breadth of spirit shows in comments spread through his descriptions of Russia: he was unusually warm about the Christian beliefs and practices of the Russians, but still prepared to critique what they did.[15] His fairness comes across when he reminded his readers that the Bible was read more widely in Russia than was generally assumed.[16] The same breadth of vision was shown in a sermon preached at St George's church, Jerusalem in the 1890s when he urged unity amongst Christians and mutual respect. The solution, interestingly, was to pray for the Holy Spirit to pour out his love:

Oh, for an outpouring of the Holy Ghost until hearts overflow to one another in love! There is no other solution of these difficulties but the yielding to the full possession of the Spirit's power. The spirit of condemnation and criticism in our church, at home and abroad, will be flooded out with the spirit of love.[17]

---

10 *With Russian Pilgrims*, p viii, p 252.
11 See the wonderful route map in *With Russian Pilgrims*, between pp 10 and 11, his comments in the Preface, p vii, and the inclusion of a history of those early voyages in an Appendix.
12 *With Russian Pilgrims*, pp 40–42 and p 255.
13 *With Russian Pilgrims*, p 54.
14 *To Kairwan the Holy*, p 120.
15 Whilst appreciating the place of icons he is unhappy about images of God, *With Russian Pilgrims*, p 250.
16 *With Russian Pilgrims*, p 252f.
17 *Days in Galilee*, p 341.

Boddy's sense of adventure and confidence in his own abilities, his ease with people from many backgrounds, and his willingness to learn from other Christians whilst being secure in his own beliefs, were used later in his life in giving leadership to the Pentecostal Movement.

His evangelistic and pastoral concerns caused him to arrange parish missions, and it was through such a mission in 1890 that he met Mary Pollock who became his wife a year later. She came as a helper on the mission and must have made a good impression on Boddy. They had much in common. Both had a clergy father; both had valued the Keswick Convention and they shared a burning desire to bring others to the Saviour they loved. Boddy appreciated Mary as a partner in ministry, for she had musical ability, teaching and pastoral skills and gifts of healing.

The Missing Link: Power from on High

Boddy was not just a great physical traveller, but also a spiritual searcher, wanting to go deeper with God, whether at home in Monkwearmouth or in other parts of the world where God seemed to be at work.

He made two significant steps forward in 1892. He realized what was missing in his spiritual experience was the personal appropriation of justification by faith. Prayer with a visiting missionary gave him confidence that his sins were forgiven and he felt he had 'a real message to give.' But this was not enough for him: 'I still longed for more power with souls, and God showed me that he was willing to fill me with his Holy Spirit because he had commanded me to be filled (Ephesians 5.18).' He then goes on to describe how God met him in a profound way during a service of Holy Communion:

> It was on the 21st September, 1892, at about 8.40 in the morning, in All Saints Church, Monkwearmouth…that the Holy Spirit in infinite love came upon me…It overwhelmed me; my voice broke, and tears were in my eyes. I knew he had come, and that I was "fulfilled with his grace and heavenly benediction."[18]

Besides his own experience of the Spirit in 1892, he and Mary were profoundly influenced by her healing from asthma in 1899. As a result Mary discovered she had a gift of healing and regularly prayed with and laid hands on sick people. Alexander did not have the gift of healing but used a service of Anointing the Sick and taught on the subject of healing. Thus they were pioneers in the movement for spiritual healing, even before their main 'Pentecostal' experience.[19]

By about 1900 the energy Boddy had previously been putting into his foreign travels was going into developing his understanding of the work of the

---

18 'The Writer's Testimony' *Confidence*, Vol 2.4, 1909, p 98.
19 Details are given in Jane Boddy's letter to Robinson, reported in Robinson *Boddy*, p 31.

Spirit. He wrote a series of twelve 'Roker Tracts' on spiritual renewal including one entitled *The Holy Ghost for us*, later reprinted in *Confidence* magazine. This tract suggests that he began with and maintained for some time an understanding of the work of the Holy Spirit as a two-stage process. He identified the gift of the Spirit spoken of in John 20.22 and Luke 24.33 with regeneration, whilst that in Acts 2 he saw as leading to sanctification.[20] This would seem to be an early version of what has become the classic Pentecostal understanding of baptism in the Holy Spirit.[21] However, he did not abandon Anglican ways and he wrote a short book for young people getting confirmed, putting it in a very positive light as a basis for Christian living, and including a defence of infant baptism, and the Creeds.[22]

His travelling now became more focussed: in 1904, when the Welsh Revival broke out, Boddy visited Ton-y-Pandy to see for himself what was happening. He was most impressed and returned to Sunderland with the news. People were said to be aglow for two years afterwards and Boddy was inspired to start a prayer meeting for further revival with 'a little circle of earnest young men.'[23]

News of the events in Wales came to Los Angeles in April 1905 and led to prayer for revival. In April 1906 people began to speak in tongues at meetings held in Asuza Street. Many people were deeply affected by the Asuza Street meetings and its influence spread throughout the USA through individual contact and its magazine *The Apostolic Faith*. A copy of the first issue was received by a Norwegian Methodist pastor, T B Barratt, who was visiting New York. After exchanging encouraging letters with the Azusa Street leaders, he met with other people in New York and himself received the gift of tongues. In December he returned to Oslo, where he held meetings to spread the Pentecostal Outpouring, as it was being called.

News of these events in Asuza Street and Oslo reached Boddy and in March 1907 he visited Barratt's meetings in Oslo for four days. His time in Oslo was hugely important, and described in a number of ways subsequently. In 1907 he called it 'a great inflow of his Spirit,' in 1908 a 'wonderful anointing of the Holy Spirit,' and in 1910 a 'blessed and wonderful "Baptism" of the Holy Ghost.' He did not speak in tongues, though, but by 1914 he was to write, 'It was one of about seven occasions in my life when I felt the presence of God and his touch in a very marked way.'[24] Whatever it was to be called, it was clearly what Boddy had been hoping and praying for. On his return home Boddy began to make preparations for Barratt to visit his parish, in the hope that Pentecost might come to Sunderland.

20   'The Holy Ghost for us' *Confidence*, Vol 5.1, 1912, p 19.
21   See the discussion in Max Turner, *Baptism in the Holy Spirit* (Grove Renewal booklet R2, 2000).
22   *The Laying on of Hands* (SPCK, 1895)
23   Later reported in *Confidence*, Vol 3.8, 1910, p 193f.
24   'Some Sacred Memories' *Confidence*, Vol 7, No 2, 1914, p 25.

2
'Pentecost' at Sunderland[25]

The Visit of Barratt to Sunderland

Alexander Boddy worked hard to get Barratt to come to Sunderland, repeatedly pressing him to come. Meanwhile, Boddy continued with prayer meetings and contacting friends. He also attended the Keswick Convention in the summer of 1907 and distributed thousands of copies of a leaflet *Pentecost for England*. Through this activity a high level of expectancy was raised, and apparently one young man had already received the gift of the Holy Spirit at a prayer meeting at All Saints Vicarage.[26]

Barratt arrived in Monkwearmouth on 31st August 1907. On the next day, a Sunday, afternoon and evening meetings were held. Barratt spoke to the congregation after Evensong and those who wanted went into an 'after meeting' in the Vestry, with the express intention of receiving the Holy Spirit. Barratt wrote ecstatically about how the first 'Baptisms in the Spirit' occurred and the meeting lasted until 4am,[27] whilst Boddy was less demonstrative and gave more details: '...two who were seeking him entered right in and went right through into Pentecost with signs following; to encourage others God allowed them to be dealt with tenderly.'[28] This pattern of two meetings a day continued, with a gradual rather than dramatic build-up of interest and numbers. Initially the visitors were nearly all believers though by 19th September Barratt noted that interest amongst outsiders was growing. But he was not seeing a repetition of the large-scale conversions he had seen in Norway. The meetings may have begun in a gentle way, to encourage others, but soon more extreme events were occurring, as Barratt recorded in his diary:

> A young man who was preparing to be a school master was also filled that same evening. He began by shouting 'Glory!' continuously...In one case the tongues came very slowly as I have noticed it sometimes in Scandinavia. All kinds of strange sounds. A stranger would have thought it like the quacking of a duck and the barking of a dog.[29]

Amongst the earliest recipients of the Baptism in the Spirit, as evidenced by the gift of tongues, were Mary Boddy who began singing in the Spirit on 11th September, and their daughters Mary and Jane on 21st September.[30] Alexan-

---

25 The title of Mary Boddy's testimony of Sept 1907, immediately following her Baptism in the Spirit.
26 *Confidence* 9.10, 1916, p 169.
27 T B Barratt, *Erindringer*, 1941, p 168.
28 *Tongues in Sunderland* (Leaflets on 'Tongues' No 9) p 1.
29 *Diary*, pp 5, 8.
30 Mary Boddy, *'Pentecost' at Sunderland: the Testimony of a Vicar's Wife*, pp 5–7.

der himself did not speak in tongues until 2nd December after Barratt had left. Even by then numbers were not huge and Boddy estimated he was the fifti- eth person to receive the gift. *Possors this*

The number of people attending the meetings grew when newspapers took an interest. According to the *Sunderland Echo* on 30th September about 100 people, mostly women, attended the open meeting and about 30 stayed for the 'after meeting.' The London papers picked up the story and press interest rocketed, especially in what were seen as the more spectacular aspects. Barratt was not bothered by the implication of notoriety, but Boddy was concerned.[31]

It was not just the newspapers. An itinerant preacher Reader Harris, leader of the Pentecostal League, was holding meetings in Sunderland at the same time as Barratt's visit to All Saints. Harris was disturbed by what he saw as extreme emotion and immoral conduct generated by the meetings led by Barratt and he attacked the outpouring as a Satanic counterfeit. Harris spoke of 'confusion, errors of conduct, and the loosening of the marriage tie.…Errors of conduct is a mild term to describe the rolling on the floor of women and men from which all true believers and indeed all decent people, should hold aloof.'[32] Barratt replied forcibly and a split ensued.

Much of the controversy arose from the emphasis Barratt placed on peo- ple receiving the gift of tongues as evidence for the Baptism in the Holy Spirit.[33] Boddy himself seemed to believe that there had been too much emphasis on tongues. His descriptions of Baptism in the Holy Spirit consistently refer to the fruit of love as the evidence, whether from this period, his earliest refer- ence to the gift of the Spirit in 1892 or the reflections of his final years. Over- all, though, Boddy remained convinced of Barratt's message and continued the special meetings after Barratt left on 18th October 1907. The meetings had become both famous and notorious with local and national publicity, but with little support for them from other church leaders. 'Much would now depend on the leadership of Alexander Alfred Boddy.'[34]

The Sunderland Conventions 1908–1914

Boddy's leadership of the Pentecostal Movement in Britain was exercised through his writing ministry and most importantly through the annual Whitsuntide Sunderland Conventions. These were held from 1908 to 1914, when the First World War brought them to a halt. Boddy's qualities of adven- ture and self-confidence, his ease with people from many backgrounds, and his willingness to learn from other Christians whilst being secure in his own beliefs, now came to the fore. Harnessed to his pastoral and evangelistic ex- perience from over twenty-five years of parish ministry these qualities gave the fledgling movement enough security to become established.

---

31 *Confidence* 3.8, 1910, p 195.
32 'The Gift of Tongues,' *Tongues of Fire*, 17.203, Nov 1907, pp 1f.
33 On Barratt see Nils Bloch-Hoell, *The Pentecostal Movement* (Allen and Unwin, 1964) p 67.
34 Robinson, *Boddy*, p 63.

Visitors had continued to come to Sunderland after Barratt had gone, including Pentecostal speakers from the USA and British leaders. The most notable of the British visitors in 1907 was Smith Wigglesworth, a plumber from Bradford who led an independent mission and had developed a powerful healing ministry. Nevertheless he desired a deeper experience of God and in November he visited the Boddys. When Mary Boddy laid hands on him in the vicarage kitchen he received a vision of the empty cross and Jesus glorified and then the gift of tongues.[35] News of such events spread quickly, encouraging people in other centres to pray still more fervently. At the beginning of January 1908 Boddy spoke at Kilsyth, Edinburgh, leading to the setting up of a key Pentecostal assembly. Contacts like these led to the first Convention in Sunderland from 6th–11th June 1908.

The Pentecostal Convention attracted participants from all over Great Britain and several European countries. Their successful organization owed much to Boddy's efficiency and ability to bring together people from different backgrounds. As chairman he had strict rules which were printed on the tickets and firmly enforced. These included accepting the rulings of the chairman, punctuality at the meetings, and allowing the leader to control the singing.

The meetings involved teaching from Boddy and others, congregational singing, and opportunities for prayer which sometimes led to extreme responses. There was a warm atmosphere and in later Conventions Boddy gave prominence to Church of England services. In 1912 there were Sunday services of Communion at 7am, 8am and 10.30am.

Many key leaders attended the first Convention, including the wealthy Cecil Polhill, one of the missionary 'Cambridge Seven,' T B Barratt, and Pastor Polman from Amsterdam. In succeeding years virtually all the future Pentecostal leaders of Britain attended, some receiving a personal Baptism in the Holy Spirit there. From Germany Pastor Paul of Berlin and Pastor Meyer of Hamburg attended and became firm friends of Boddy.

Boddy's age and long ministry in Sunderland gave respectability to what might have been seen as an extremist movement. By 1910 numbers were such that people were forced onto the streets and there was national press interest with a brief report in *The Times*,[36] and photographs in the *Daily Mirror*.[37] In 1911 it was reported that some local ministers were attending, and by 1912 the Convention was opened by the Mayor of Sunderland in his chain of office.

The Conventions became important in bringing together and encouraging the early Pentecostal Movement in Britain and Europe. However, the growth in the Movement was putting strain on Boddy's leadership and problems of discipline began to emerge. The success of the meetings was generating more emotion and expectation and in 1913 and particularly 1914 there were break-

---

35 Colin Whittaker, *Seven Pentecostal Pioneers* (Marshall, Morgan and Scott, 1983) pp 21–27 provides helpful details including two letters from Wigglesworth to the Boddys.
36 18th May 1910, p 4.
37 'General Booth's Brother-in-law at the Pentecostal Convention' 8th June 1911, p 6.

downs in order and outbursts of speaking in tongues with which Boddy was not happy, not least because of all the newspaper reporters now present.

Even more significantly for the future—remember Boddy was 60 years old in 1914—Pentecostalism was developing independently of other church groups. Although Boddy himself wanted to see the Pentecostal Movement work within the existing churches, this was not possible in most places and younger leaders formed new groups. Baptismal ceremonies in the sea were carried out at the Conventions, not by the official leadership but nonetheless using the name of the Conventions. It began with a single candidate in 1912 and even this small scale ceremony was reported in the *Newcastle Daily Journal*.[38] The following year Smith Wigglesworth baptized three women and two men in the sea, an event reported nationally.[39] By 1914 such baptisms were frequent and it was clear that Boddy's leadership would have been considerably weakened even without the catastrophe of the First World War.

In assessing the importance of the Sunderland Conventions it is worth hearing from Pentecostal historians. The first British Pentecostal historian, Donald Gee, wrote that these Conventions 'must occupy the supreme place in importance' in the early life of the Pentecostal Movement in British Isles.[40] The British Pentecostal historian, William Kay, endorses Gee's view and adds his own positive assessment of Boddy himself: 'The conventions were held in Boddy's parish and he was their dignified and respected chairman.'[41]

Confidence *magazine*

The publication of the magazine *Confidence* with Boddy as editor and chief contributor was also very important. The magazine made great use of sermons and lectures given at the Conventions, whilst attendance at the Conventions benefited from the publicity provided by the magazines. Its circulation has been estimated at about 6,000 copies each month, and Boddy claimed it went to every part of the English-speaking world.[42]

A typical issue contained a great variety of items, often jumbled together. The first substantial item was usually a long piece by Boddy, sometimes describing his travels and encounters with Christians elsewhere. Sometimes it was a reflective or devotional piece. In many issues Mary wrote a devotional and theological article. Teaching from other people was included, especially sermons and talks given at the annual Conventions. There was news of events in the Pentecostal Movement around the world, comments about books, and some reflection on wider issues, notably the First World War. Several pages were devoted to the work of the Pentecostal Missionary Union (PMU).

38   *Newcastle Daily Journal*, 1st May 1912, p 7.
39   *Daily Sketch*, 'Baptized in pale blue pyjamas,' p 6; *Daily Mirror*, p 1 and 'Converts Icy Bath,' p 5, all on 16th May 1913.
40   Donald Gee, *Wind and Flame* (AOG Publishing House, 1967) p 37.
41   William Kay, *Pentecostals in Britain* (Paternoster Press, 2000) p 12.
42   William Kay, *Inside Story* (Mattersey Hall Publishing, 1990) p 31.

Through it all, one is aware that the editor was in charge as a benevolent autocrat, and his gentle firmness comes across.

Confidence remained important until the early 1920s when other publications from the Pentecostal Movement began to take its place. It faded away as Boddy himself grew tired and became peripheral to the Movement.

Spreading the Word Abroad

Boddy's experience as a traveller gave him the impetus to take the Pentecostal message abroad. The Sunderland Conventions were themselves international, the magazine *Confidence* was widely circulated and Boddy spread the Pentecostal message through personal contact.

The first tangible sign was the setting up of the PMU in January 1909. The prime mover was Cecil Polhill, who had previously supported the China Inland Mission, and he became the secretary and treasurer. The first council meeting was in the All Saints vicarage and Boddy became the editorial secretary. Publicity came out through *Confidence* until the penultimate issue in 1925, when reports were moved to *Redemption Tidings*.[43]

The council of the PMU asked other Pentecostal centres to send representatives and names of candidates for foreign service, as well as offerings to finance the work. The reputation of Boddy and the Sunderland Convention —there had only been one at this stage—was already such that they could assume the leadership of the Pentecostal Movement. Boddy had no desire to create a Pentecostal denomination, but the existence of the PMU showed his ability to set up a national network centred on Sunderland and using the magazine *Confidence*. Just a little later he wrote:

> The Writer has felt strongly that it is a mistake to form another home organization, which soon may become another 'church,' and follow the fate of so many before it. Union for the purpose of sending out and helping and advising Pentecostal Missionaries in the dark places of Heathenism, is to his mind, the great need today.[44]

From 1909 the Sunderland Conventions were known as the International Conference and included time for PMU business. Boddy continued his visits to mainland Europe and North America, and helped found a PMU in the USA.[45]

Barratt has rightly been seen as the apostle of the Pentecostal Movement in Europe because of his long and early ministry,[46] but Boddy influenced Barratt's own understanding and helped to create a European network of Pentecostal leaders. Boddy was a key member of the International Advisory Council (IAC) as it tackled the position of speaking in tongues, the organisa-

---

43 *Confidence* 141, 1926, p 8.
44 *Confidence* 2.8, 1909, p 175.
45 *Confidence* 2.8, 1909, p 174f.
46 Bloch-Hoell p 75, citing also David du Plessis and Donald Gee.

tion of the Movement, and countering extremism.

The German pastors wanted to minimize the significance of speaking in tongues as the sign of Baptism in the Holy Spirit, over against Barratt and his supporters who saw this as denial of the Pentecostal Movement. Boddy himself was indebted to Barratt and from early on promoted the value of speaking in tongues. However, he did not regard tongues as sufficient proof of Baptism in the Spirit, and he repeatedly emphasized the importance of divine love and Christ-like lives. Boddy's description of his own first experience of the Holy Spirit in 1892 also emphasized divine love as the first fruit, and this was a consistent theme in his teaching.[47] After years of debate this was effectively the position accepted by the IAC of December 1912.

There were similar lines of division over the best form of organization. Barratt wanted to create a new denomination, but he was opposed by the Germans and Boddy, consistent with his actions over the PMU. Boddy's view was summarized in his editorial 'Unity not Uniformity'[48] and again his view prevailed at the IAC meeting of 1912.

Finally, all the leaders were agreed in wanting to guard against what they saw as extreme teaching, though of course the Pentecostal teaching was itself seen as extreme by other Christians. As a pastor, more than a diplomat or missionary, Boddy was very appreciative of Europe's Christian heritage, as his travel books showed, and not just western Europe. He saw the Pentecostal task as being to preserve and restore that heritage rather than build a new ecclesiastical empire.[49]

His concerns in North America were somewhat different. He was not impressed by the state of religious life in USA, though he thought the Pentecostal people were orthodox in belief. He made three visits before the First World War, apparently at the invitation and financing of American friends. He went on long journeys, including a visit to Azusa Street, and to many denominational churches especially the Episcopal sister churches to the Church of England, and he visited both black and white congregations.

In the USA Boddy acted more as an evangelist, both for the gospel and for the Pentecostal Movement to existing denominations. He was concerned to discover 'where ever I went it was money, money much more than Christ.'[50] He was also very concerned about 'the colour problem,' and hoped that Pentecostal witness might overcome such divisions.[51] Because he found the record of American churches to be weak over the issues of money and racism he was prepared to speak against the status quo: as in his urban ministry in Sunderland he continued to be motivated by a concern for equality.[52]

47 *Confidence*, No 1, 1908, p 18; 2.2 1909, p 33; *Confidence* 3.11 1910, p 261.
48 *Confidence* 4.3, 1911, p 60.
49 *Confidence* 2.11, 1909, p 263.
50 *Confidence* 5.10, 1912, p 223.
51 The Baptism of the Spirit had been seen as overcoming barriers of colour at Asuza Street in 1907.
52 *Confidence* 5.11, 1912, p 244f.

3

Later Life

First World War Trauma

Boddy heard of the possibility of war with Germany whilst on his third trip to USA. It meant the cancellation of the 1915 Convention, being replaced by a small local event over the Whitsun weekend and by a larger Convention in London. The Convention was moved partly because of fears of an invasion of the north east coast, and partly because the war effort was important to Boddy—the Parish Hall was being used as a detention hospital for the forces.[53] During the war years, Cecil Polhill became the convenor of the Conventions. Boddy still spoke, but the move diminished his position and the pre-eminence of Sunderland in British Pentecostalism. At first Boddy continued to publish *Confidence* as before but by 1917 it had had to become bi-monthly.

Boddy's attitude to the war was a complex mixture of heartfelt patriotism and distress at the break in Christian fellowship with other European Pentecostal leaders. Initially he was shocked about the war, then he found it 'almost unthinkable' to be separated from Pentecostal friends in Germany.[54] Boddy felt they were misinformed and was distressed to learn of forty German Pentecostals who were fighting.[55] German Pentecostals were more uniformly patriotic than British Pentecostals, which prevented the splits that later occurred in Britain within the Pentecostal Movement. Boddy himself was very supportive of the war effort, aware of his position as a Church of England clergyman. He urged all Pentecostal assemblies to join a night of prayer on 28th November 1914 to repent of sin and to ask for victory.[56] The following year he visited troops and stressed his sympathy and role as an Anglican priest.

However, many British Pentecostals were Conscientious Objectors, including Donald Gee and Howard Carter, and some were imprisoned for their belief. This conflict of views is reflected in the pages of *Confidence*. Boddy does mention an anti-war book by A S Booth-Clibborn, but he makes it clear that he does not agree and recommends F Ballard's *Britain Justified—The War from the Christian Standpoint*.[57] Boddy's views, shared by Polhill, increased the gulf between them and the younger leaders. Gee suggests the imprisonment was persecution for their beliefs as Pentecostals not just as Christians.[58]

At the same time, separate Elim churches began to grow through George Jeffreys. In 1917 Boddy mentions the expulsion of Pastor Saxby from his Bap-

---

53 *The North Star*, 24th May 1915, p 2.
54 *Confidence* 7.9, 1914, p 163.
55 *Confidence* 7.10, 1914, p 191.
56 *ibid*.
57 *Confidence* 8.1, 1915, p 6.
58 Gee, *Wind and Flame*, p 102.

tist church.[59] The shoots of separate organisations were becoming visible, a growth which Boddy had sought to resist, but was now powerless to do so. Cecil Polhill speaking at the 1917 Conference continued to emphasize world evangelisation as essential but the leadership of British Pentecostalism was inexorably passing to other people.[60] Revival within the churches had not happened and pressure was growing for a new direction.

Boddy's Latter Years

For a brief moment it looked as if Boddy might take up his leadership after the war when he had an invitation to speak from USA and Canada. But his passport was refused in the post-war confusion and no further invitation came.

Similarly when Polhill decided not to convene the 1919 conference the task fell not to Boddy but to Pastor Saxby. Boddy did attend and he also spoke at the next three Conferences (1920–22) but although Polhill was the convenor again from 1920–24 the break had been important. Under Polhill's leadership the London meetings became less overtly 'Pentecostal,' with characteristics such as prophecy and speaking in tongues more restrained. The emphasis was on encouraging foreign missionary work through the PMU. Donald Gee tells the story of a PMU missionary interrupting a meeting with a message in tongues. It was listened to but, he believed, more with embarrassment than in a 'truly Pentecostal atmosphere'.[61]

By the early 1920s Boddy was becoming less involved in the new directions the Pentecostal Movement was taking. He spoke at his last Convention in 1922. *Confidence* had been quarterly since 1918, and it petered out after 1924. In 1924 the Assemblies of God was formed and Boddy and Polhill left the council of the PMU. Apart from two further short editions of *Confidence*, that was the end of Boddy's public involvement with Pentecostalism.

In the same period the Boddys finally left Sunderland. In December 1922, they moved to the village of Pittington, a few miles east of Durham. Here they hoped for healthier conditions away from the industry of Sunderland. So many people came to his farewell service of Holy Communion, including many non-conformists, that a second service had to be held. Here was a final testimony to the Boddys' long and faithful ministry in this working-class parish.

In his new country parish he continued his energetic work, soon visiting all his parishioners on his bicycle. He built up the life of the church community, re-introducing confirmation and developing the choir. Although Mary was largely housebound with painful arthritis, she did still manage to run a men's Bible class in 1927 and continued with her healing ministry. In October that year she became seriously ill, dying on 25th April 1928. Alexander lived a little longer, supported in his ministry by his daughter Jane, until he became ill himself in the summer of 1930 and died on 30th September.

---

59 *Confidence* 10.4, 1917, p 56.
60 *Confidence* 10.3, 1917, p 35.
61 Gee, *Wind and Flame*, p 111.

4
Theology and Practice

This chapter sets out the main theological issues of significance to Boddy himself. Boddy was nurtured in the Holiness Movement, which had a very high view of Scripture. He included articles in *Confidence* on the authority and inspiration of the Bible, which he saw as indispensable for Christians. This approach to the Bible naturally ran though all his theological understanding but it did not make him narrow-minded. He was very much a pastor who cared for people and wanted 'God's best' for them; his theology should therefore be read in the light of his pastoral concerns.

The Centrality of Christ

The last edition of *Confidence* Boddy produced in Sunderland included a long article headed simply 'A Personal Testimony,' with information about his own life and theology. Significantly he ends the piece with a description of how the Holy Spirit has led him to see the central place of Christ: 'For he has taught me not to place him—the Holy Spirit—in the place of Christ, but to allow him to glorify Christ in us and through us. It is Christ alone who saves.'[62]

In the same issue he writes another article setting out the familiar evangelical doctrine of new birth, with a total commitment to Christ as the Saviour and to whom Christians are united by faith. The role of the Holy Spirit is to make that union real for the believer and he goes on to rejoice that there may be a time of 'rapturous joy.' However, it is clearly stated that the Christian should follow the order Fact (meaning the Fact of salvation in Christ revealed in Scripture), Faith and then Feeling. He warns that new believers are frequently tempted to reverse the order, and so become discouraged in difficult times.[63] Here is the voice of the evangelical pastor who is devoted to Christ.

'One, Holy, Catholic and Apostolic Church'

The four Credal adjectives about the church provide a good summary of Boddy's view of the church and indeed much of his theology and practice.

Boddy retained a very high view of the church throughout his life, always seeking fellowship with other Christians, and unity in witness. He saw Pentecostalism as a renewal movement within the existing churches, a view which conflicted with Barratt but was held by other European leaders in the early stages of the Movement. He described the inter-denominational nature of the Pentecostal Movement as an evidence that it was of God.[64] Thus Boddy en-

---

62 *Confidence* 131, 1922, p 56.
63 *ibid*, pp 54–6.
64 *Confidence* 3.5, 1910, p 103f.

couraged people to know Christ in the power of the Holy Spirit but he did not expect them to leave their churches, nor did he suggest that only Pentecostals were Christians.[65] In his own parish Pentecostal prayer meetings were held on Friday, Saturday and Sunday evenings for a number of years but they were not the only activities and they were not held with any exclusive intent.

Boddy had had his early Christian life revitalized by going to the Keswick Convention, the central gathering for the Holiness Movement, and his Pentecostal experience built on that earlier period of his life. He believed in personal holiness, pleading the Blood for sin and for victory over disease.[66] He also was concerned to see holiness in a wider context: he had been prepared to work for and with poor working people in his parish and on his journeys before his Pentecostal experience. Later when travelling in the USA he was troubled by the materialism and racism he saw and spoke against both, looking for Pentecostals to set good examples over these issues. For Boddy holiness was not confined to personal piety but had a corporate outworking. His support for the war effort was based on his view of the correctness of supporting helpless Belgium in the face of German militarism.[67]

Boddy exemplified belief in the church as a worldwide, universal body with his positive remarks about believers from many lands and denominations. His travels throughout his life brought him into contact with a great variety of Christians and churches and he sought to learn from them. This openness was important in his acceptance of the Pentecostal message, and enabled him to provide leadership of the Movement when other Anglicans were unable to do so.

Boddy was committed to the church as apostolic in two senses of the word: as founded historically on the commissioning and witness of the apostles by Jesus; and in its continuing missionary task. Boddy followed the Holiness Movement's strong commitment to Scripture and was concerned to teach the apostolic message. And throughout his life he was ready to witness to his belief in Christ, and held regular parish missions. He was a great supporter of CMS, both when abroad and through parish support groups.

Spiritual gifts

Boddy had enormous influence on the understanding of spiritual gifts in the twentieth century. It is right therefore to address this issue immediately following his ecclesiology, since he saw spiritual gifts in the context of the church, as building up the church, encouraging believers, and helping them to live holy lives. Kay's recent history of British Pentecostalism begins its theological survey of spiritual gifts with Boddy and the Sunderland Conventions. In assessing current Pentecostal beliefs about vocal spiritual gifts, he

---

65 See Robinson, *Boddy* p 116.
66 *Confidence*, No 5, 1908, p 5.
67 *Confidence* 8.1, 1915, p 4.

concludes that 'the main outlines of understanding have remained largely intact' from those of the Conventions.[68]

The fullest discussions of spiritual gifts in the pages of *Confidence* are found on the topics of speaking in tongues, prophecy and on healing, and all were discussed at the first Convention.

Speaking in Tongues

In the first issue of *Confidence* Boddy wrote that 'tongues is a Seal of Pentecost.'[69] He did not see it as absolutely necessary for Baptism in the Holy Spirit, and, quoting 1 Cor 12.29, he distinguished this initial blessing from the continuing gift of tongues. He also expected there to be fruit—not service as for later Pentecostals, but rather love.

On a number of occasions Boddy summarized his teaching on tongues, which suggests it continued to be controversial. In 1910 he printed his address to a Men's Service in St Gabriel's Sunderland, in which he explained the use of tongues in prayer and adoration. He went through the scriptural passages relating to tongues and gave present day examples. Throughout, his emphasis was on the value of tongues and the greater importance of exalting Jesus and following him.[70]

Prophecy

Boddy wanted potential prophets to have letters of commendation from well-known leaders to avoid 'unsuitable persons' which suggests he was alert to possible problems, and this coheres with his general concern that the Pentecostal Movement be as well received as possible.[71] From the beginning he was clear that messages in tongues and prophecies were not to be expected to give guidance in everyday life, though 'at any crisis…God can and does give a special message.'[72] Guidance came about through 'common sense' under God's control.

In 1911 Boddy published a talk by Pastor Paul from the Whitsuntide Convention concentrating on prophecy as being to exhort, edify and comfort, and leaving on one side more apocalyptic understandings.[73] A further discussion on the ministry of women in 1914 wrestled with biblical texts which referred to women both prophesying and keeping silent, and their own experience of women prophesying. The general conclusions were that women could prophesy in smaller gatherings, distinguished from the church assembly, and that it should be carried out under the authority of a male pastor.[74]

68   Kay, *Pentecostals in Britain*, p 79.
69   *Confidence*, No 1, 1908, p 18.
70   *Confidence* 3.5, 1910, pp 99–104.
71   *Confidence*, No 3, 1908, p 15.
72   *ibid*, p 13.
73   *Confidence* 4.11, 1911, p 249 .
74   *Confidence* 7.11, 1914, pp 209, 212–214.

Healing

The healing of Mary Boddy from asthma in 1899 was crucial in making Boddy open to Pentecostal phenomena. It seems to have arisen from Mary's own reflections on Scripture whilst laid up, for in her testimony she wrote:

> I was willing, if it were God's will, to be an invalid—not having heard of Divine Healing. I began to search the Scriptures on this point, relying on the Holy Spirit to teach me...After many months of prayer, God *spoke* to me from John 5.39–40, on the 23rd of February, 1899, and as I believed the Word and *received* Jesus to come into me as my physical life, he did so, and I was made whole.[75] [italics hers]

Mary then discovered she had a gift of healing and would regularly lay hands on people, and their daughter Jane records that this was the normal practice in cases of sickness within her own family.[76]

This makes all the more interesting Kay's assessment that Boddy developed a balanced view on healing which helped later Pentecostalism.[77] His many years of experience ensured a reality about claims for healing. The first issue of *Confidence* included a discussion of healing, and the second an overview article by Mary on 'Health and Healing.' Theologically she located healing in the atonement. Alexander himself referred to James 5.14, the laying on of hands and the gift of healing, but not the atonement. He expressed a rounded view of healing, writing of the importance of prayer, the use of oil, salvation of body, soul and spirit and the importance of not exaggerating testimonies of healing.[78] The theology of healing was never systematized by Boddy, but he stressed its reality without rejecting conventional medicine. He accepted that few people would have the faith to rely solely on God for healing.

Sacraments

Boddy retained his evangelical Anglican stance on baptism and Holy Communion throughout his life, a fact which caused some conflict within the Pentecostal Movement.

His support for infant baptism remains somewhat sensitive to Pentecostals; for example, an Elim author Richard Bicknell has written of 'the sacramentalist position of the early "fathers,"'[79] clearly including Boddy in this assessment. Differences of opinion over the baptism of infants is recorded in *Confidence*, and, although Boddy himself did want it, the issue does seem to have been a factor in the gradual separation of Pentecostals from the established churches.

It is also clear from his practice that Boddy took Communion very seriously. The programme for the first Whitsuntide Conference in 1908 included

---

75 Mary Boddy, *Testimony*, p 2.
76 Jane Boddy letter to Martin Robinson 1975, p 5.
77 Kay, *Pentecostals in Britain*, p 82.
78 *Confidence*, No 3, 1908, p 18.
79 Richard Bicknell, 'The Ordinances' in Keith Warrington (ed), *Pentecostal Perspectives* (Paternoster, 1998), p 214.

two celebrations of Holy Communion on Whitsunday,[80] and in 1912 there were three services, beginning at 7am, which many of the Conference participants attended.[81] Furthermore, his earliest conscious experience of the Holy Spirit in 1892 occurred at an early morning service of communion to celebrate St Matthew's Day.[82]

However, there is nothing within his writings to suggest that his views on the sacraments were significantly different from other evangelical Anglicans. The differences with other Pentecostals arose mainly because of the previously held beliefs of each party.

The Second Coming of Christ

Boddy held an apocalyptic eschatology of a kind common at the time. He had a strong sense that Christ could return soon, a view which pre-dated his Pentecostal experience. So when preaching in Jerusalem in the 1890s he concluded his sermon with reference to the Second Coming of Christ, which, like others, he believed would take place on the Mount of Olives.[83] Receiving the baptism of the Holy Spirit reinforced this belief, and amongst a handful of key doctrines printed at the front of *Confidence* for a number of years he included 'the Soon-Coming of the Lord in the air (1 Thess 4.14).'[84] It was his hope that Pentecostal revival would lead to a restoring of the unity of the church and an end to unbelief, so hastening the return of the Lord. His belief in an imminent *parousia* gave urgency to missionary work, which was done through the PMU and sharing the gospel at home.

He took note of supposed prophesies which sought to determine when the return of Christ might occur, but argued against this approach, using the text, 'But of that day and hour knoweth no man' (Matthew 24.36). Nonetheless, he saw the outbreak of war in 1914 as a sign of the 'end times.' In January 1915, hearing of an earthquake in Rome, he used Luke 21.10–11 as the heading for a short report.[85] Later in the same issue Mary wrote 'The end of the age is at hand' and described the signs of spiritual conflict which were the evidence. The following month a long article on The War began with a discussion of Armageddon and saw the declaration of war by Turkey, with soldiers marching across Syria, as at least a possible fulfilment of Revelation 19.19.[86]

These selections show how important the topic was to him. Its importance was strengthened by his personal experience of the Holy Spirit, giving a sense of the closeness of God, and then by the trauma of the 1914–18 war which was reminiscent of the apocalyptic visions of the New Testament.

---

80 *Confidence*, No 2, May 1908, p 2.
81 *Confidence* 5.6, June 1912, p 126.
82 See chapter 1.
83 *Days in Galilee*, p 343.
84 *Confidence*, April 1911–Jan/Feb 1917.
85 *Confidence*, Jan 1915, p 8.
86 *Confidence*, Feb 1915, p 26.

5

The Legacy of Alexander Boddy

Boddy's contribution to the development of Pentecostalism is beginning to be more widely acknowledged. Within Sunderland itself a local history study was published in 1986. The church of All Saints has had a returning awareness of its own history, partly sparked by the sale of the church hall used for many Pentecostal meetings to the Monkwearmouth Christian Fellowship in 1996.[87] The Fellowship's new notice board states this is 'The Birthplace of British Pentecostalism.' In the same period a group associated with the Assemblies of God formed the Sunderland Christian Centre, also explicitly drawing inspiration from the ministry of Boddy.[88] Pentecostal historians, beginning with Donald Gee, have given Boddy honourable mention. His importance has also been recognized by the publication of *Confidence* on CD-ROM by the Assemblies of God in the USA.

The Contribution Made by Boddy
Leadership

Boddy had considerable authority as a leader, taking up the position through organizing the Conventions and publishing *Confidence*. The tone of his instructions concerning behaviour at the first Conference meetings leaves no doubt as to where the human authority lay. However, it is not correct to describe him as an 'aristocrat,'[89] but more accurately as a university educated member of the Victorian middle class. He became a solicitor without a law degree, and did not attend Oxford or Cambridge because he and his father could not afford the fees.

In fact, he was described as humble and warm, and even in the 1980s there were people who remembered him with affection, and not as a domineering man. The evidence of his travel writing is of a confident person, but also one who is open to learn from others and their circumstances. That confidence and openness was used to the full in his search for Holiness and his subsequent promotion of Pentecostalism.

His considerable organizational skills were fully used in the running and delegation of the practical arrangements of the Whitsuntide Conventions. The smooth running of the Conventions and their regularity was a major contribution to the cohesion and development of Pentecostalism in Britain and Europe. There were other gatherings during this period but the Sunderland meetings were the most important.

---

87 A development from the Elim fellowship.
88 Ken and Lois Gott, *The Sunderland Refreshing* (Hodder & Stoughton, 1995) p 75.
89 W J Hollenweger *Pentecostalism* (Hendrickson,1997) p 344.

Teaching and Pastoral Concern

Boddy's teachings were disseminated through his Roker Tracts before his Pentecostal experience of 1907 and his teaching went far wider in *Confidence*. He may not have always agreed fully with every point made, for example, in articles critical of the war effort, but reading the magazine one is left with the impression that it is largely Boddy's own position that is being expressed. The teaching that he gave and promoted is traceable down to the present day, and that alone would have given him a prominent position in the history of Pentecostalism.

Boddy brought a very strong sense of care about people to all his ministry, and almost everything he wrote expresses his concern for their well-being, spiritual, physical and social. When it came to Pentecostal experience he was firm in insisting that the use of spiritual gifts was for the upbuilding of the church and the good of the people. Any attempt to manipulate people was frowned upon, and his care can be seen in the meticulous recording of who had experienced what. He did not want to exaggerate the effects of the Movement and played down the more extreme manifestations associated with revival meetings, though nor did he want 'to quench the Spirit.'[90] In the USA he spoke at black churches as well as white, and rejoiced in fellowship between black and white Christians, seeing very clearly the implications of Christian fellowship for breaking down barriers between nations, cultures and different Christian traditions. [91]

Boddy's Legacy

Although Boddy's vision of a renewed church had apparently failed even before the end of his life there are two ways in which he has left a lasting legacy.

His first legacy has been in the lives of people. For all his failure to develop a team of leaders he provided much needed pastoral support and wisdom to nearly all the early British Pentecostal leaders and he was a major influence amongst European leaders.

His second legacy for today's church lies in the way that he held together a Pentecostal spirituality with a range of other important contemporary concerns—Anglican practice and pastoral care, an ecumenical vision, an international vision and the social implications of faith.

Investigating and learning something of the story of this Pentecostal Anglican is therefore a reminder of the diversity of Pentecostal roots, an aid to dialogue across traditions, and may provide resources for us as we seek to hold together a similar range of concerns in our own day.

---

90   See for example *Confidence* 7.9, 1914, p 173.
91   *ibid*, p 174.

Appendix

Timeline

1854   15th November: Alexander Alfred born

1860s   Manchester Grammar School

1871   articled to R Worsley and W Parker, solicitors in Manchester
father James moved to Elwick Hall, Co Durham

1876   Toured Western Europe. Spiritual crisis at Keswick Convention.
December: admitted as solicitor by Master of the Rolls

1878   Exhibitioner at University College, Durham

1880   Awarded Licentiate in Theology. Ordained deacon by Bishop
Lightfoot. Curate to his father at Elwick Hall, Co Durham.
Visit to Sweden (or possibly in the following year)

1881   26th March: his father died. Ordained priest. Curate, St Helen's Low
Fell. Visit to S Russia and Crimea. Possibly also first visit that year to
Egypt and Holy Land

1884   Curate, St Helen's, Bishop Auckland. Curate-in-charge, All Saints,
Monkwearmouth. Visit to northern Russia?

1885   Elected Fellow of the Royal Geographical Society

1886   Vicar, All Saints, Monkwearmouth

1890   Parish mission; helpers included Mary Pollock, whose brother James
came as curate the following year

1891   Married Mary Pollock

1892   Birth of daughter, Mary (May) Vazeille. Raised £500 for ironworkers
'laid off' during Miners Strike. 21st September: 'the Holy Spirit in infi-
nite love came upon me' at an early morning Communion service

1893   birth of daughter, Jane Vazeille

1895   birth of son, James

1896   visit to Egypt

1899   23rd February: wife Mary healed of asthma, through faith in Christ

1903   5th September: his mother, Jane, died

1904   visited Welsh revival to meet Evan Roberts

1906   Asuza Street revival, Los Angeles; the usually recognized beginning
of Pentecostalism

1907   March: visited revival meetings in Oslo with T B Barratt
August: visited Keswick Convention to distribute leaflets
September–October: visit of T B Barratt to Monkwearmouth
11th September : Mary received the gift of tongues
2nd December: Alexander received the gift of tongues

1908   First Sunderland Whitsuntide Convention. 8th–11th December: attended a key Pentecostal Conference in Hamburg, Germany

1909   9th January: formation of PMU, with Boddy as Editorial Secretary

1912   Visit to USA. December: International Advisory Council

1914   Last Convention at Sunderland. June–August: visit to USA (seventh)
1914–18 European war disrupted the Pentecostal Movement
1922   Moved to Pittington
1928   25th April Death of Mary
1930   10th September death of Alexander, aged 75

Published Works by Boddy in Date Order

To Kairwan the Holy: Scenes in Muhammedan Africa (London: Kegan Paul, 1885)

With Russian Pilgrims, being an account of a sojourn in the White Sea monastery and a journey by the old trade route from the Arctic Sea to Moscow (London: Wells Gardner, Darton & Co, 1892)

The Laying on of Hands (London: SPCK, 1895)

By Ocean, Prairie and Peak: Four Journeys to British Columbia and Eastern Canada (London: SPCK, 1896)

Christ in His Holy Land: A life of Our Lord, Written During and After a Special Journey in Palestine (London: SPCK, 1897)

From the Egyptian Ramleh (London: Gay & Bird, 1900)

Days in Galilee and Scenes in Judah: Together with some Account of a Solitary Cycling Journey in Southern Palestine (London: Gay & Bird, 1900)

Roker Tracts

Confidence editor and numerous articles 1908–26

The Church of St Lawrence the Martyr, Pittington (Hallgarth), Durham (London SPCK, 1924)

Boddy Family Tree

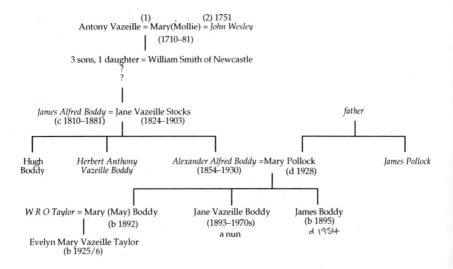

Note: Names in *italics* indicate ordained ministers